Barriers to Bankable Infrastructure

Incentivizing Private Investment to Fill the Global Infrastructure Gap

PROJECT DIRECTOR
Daniel F. Runde

PRINCIPAL AUTHOR
Helen Moser

CONTRIBUTING AUTHOR
Erin Nealer

*A Report of the CSIS Project on
U.S. Leadership in Development*

March 2016

CSIS | CENTER FOR STRATEGIC &
INTERNATIONAL STUDIES

ROWMAN &
LITTLEFIELD

Lanham • Boulder • New York • London

About CSIS

For over 50 years, the Center for Strategic and International Studies (CSIS) has worked to develop solutions to the world's greatest policy challenges. Today, CSIS scholars are providing strategic insights and bipartisan policy solutions to help decisionmakers chart a course toward a better world.

CSIS is a nonprofit organization headquartered in Washington, D.C. The Center's 220 full-time staff and large network of affiliated scholars conduct research and analysis and develop policy initiatives that look into the future and anticipate change.

Founded at the height of the Cold War by David M. Abshire and Admiral Arleigh Burke, CSIS was dedicated to finding ways to sustain American prominence and prosperity as a force for good in the world. Since 1962, CSIS has become one of the world's preeminent international institutions focused on defense and security; regional stability; and transnational challenges ranging from energy and climate to global health and economic integration.

Thomas J. Pritzker was named chairman of the CSIS Board of Trustees in November 2015. Former U.S. deputy secretary of defense John J. Hamre has served as the Center's president and chief executive officer since 2000.

CSIS does not take specific policy positions; accordingly, all views expressed herein should be understood to be solely those of the author(s).

Center for Strategic & International Studies
1616 Rhode Island Avenue, NW
Washington, DC 20036
202-887-0200 | www.csis.org

Rowman & Littlefield
4501 Forbes Boulevard
Lanham, MD 20706
301-459-3366 | www.rowman.com

Contents

Acknowledgments

The authors would like to thank the individuals who contributed to the research and review of this report. In particular this includes Conor Savoy, fellow and deputy director of the Project on Prosperity and Development and the Project on U.S. Leadership in Development at CSIS; and interns Ariel Gandolfo and Amy Chang. The authors would also like to thank the individuals representing the U.S. government, the private sector, civil society, and multilateral institutions who participated in off-the-record roundtables and interviews to inform this research. Specific thanks goes to the U.S. Trade and Development Agency (USTDA) for its contributions.

This report was made possible by Chevron Corporation's generous funding to the Project on U.S. Leadership in Development.

Executive Summary

An estimated $1 trillion annual infrastructure gap means shortfalls in services and economic bottlenecks for billions of people globally. These strains are felt especially in developing countries, where there is not a base of quality infrastructure. While U.S. government agencies and the multilateral development banks (MDBs) have been leaders in extending infrastructure to low- and middle-income countries, spending by these institutions is not near enough. There are also concerns about efficiency. Speed is typically among a partner's top priorities in implementing an infrastructure project, but completion time frames often extend far beyond estimates.

The China-led Asian Infrastructure and Investment Bank (AIIB), which opened on January 16, 2016, and is expected to begin lending by the end of the year, intensified an already heated global conversation about infrastructure. Time will tell the extent to which the AIIB is able to implement high-quality infrastructure projects in quicker time frames than the existing MDBs. In any case, the emergence of the AIIB offers a moment for reflection and action by the traditional entities on how they can prepare infrastructure projects more effectively.

Infrastructure experts have noted that within the past two years across emerging markets, including Asia, governments have called for significantly greater scale in infrastructure projects, as well as more private capital to support them. Demands for energy capacity to be built in Indonesia, Brazil, Mexico, Bangladesh, and other locales in just the next five years outstrip the current energy capacity in those places.

Given the magnitude of the capital needed to meet the global infrastructure gap, the private sector's investment in infrastructure is critical. However, private investment in infrastructure has declined in recent years. Some of this decline can be attributed to the 2008 global financial crisis, but there are other considerations that determine the private sector's willingness to invest. While many private companies are looking to support infrastructure projects led by U.S. agencies and multilateral institutions with readily available capital, they have not always found a viable project pipeline. Private actors are often dissuaded by long approval processes or perceived high financial risk at various stages of a project. Other concerns include the lack of local capacity, political will, and legal redress protection for investors; a mismatch of skills and expectations among government agencies and private-sector actors; and the mindset of MDBs to "get money out the door" and finance "low hanging fruits" can also lead to lost deals. Much can and should be done to better incentivize private participation in infrastructure.

To create a more robust pipeline of bankable infrastructure projects that attract private-sector investment, MDBs and U.S. agencies should focus on reform in main three areas: project preparation, financial products that protect investors from risk, and foreign government capacity building.

Project preparation is the critical first step of developing infrastructure projects. This often includes developing approaches toward the enabling environment, defining a project, determining project feasibility, structuring the project, providing transaction support, and developing monitoring and evaluation plans. There has been a surge in infrastructure project preparation facilities (IPPFs) in recent years. It is important these be demand and market driven so they respond to where the private sector wants to develop projects; involve the private sector early; provide grant funds for project development; focus on the development needs of a country; and emphasize technical capacity building.

Next, private-sector actors primarily seek adequate risk allocation when making investment decisions because infrastructure projects are inherently time consuming and risky. Private-sector actors look for guarantees for various stages of a project, but the innovation and evolution in both the public and private insurance industries has been largely stagnant for the last decade. New financial products are needed to greater incentivize private investment.

Finally, investors seek a strong enabling environment in which their investments can flourish. This includes legal redress protection, local capacity to implement infrastructure projects, and strong political will. Training a cadre of government officials as able and responsive counterparts early on is an important component of infrastructure strategies and projects.

Specific recommendations for U.S. agencies and MDBs include:

1. *The United States should pursue a strategic development and infrastructure finance agenda alongside its trade agenda in the Asia region, and take a stronger approach in emphasizing U.S. comparative advantages.* This should involve:
   a. Launching a major new initiative in collaboration with Japan and other allies to strengthen the Asian Development Bank (ADB).
   b. Expanding and refining global project preparation support, especially by strengthening the USTDA.
   c. Reducing the time for loan approval to a maximum of two years and no longer require guarantees from developing country recipient governments in all cases.
   d. Providing technical training and knowledge transfers in each infrastructure project.

2. *The traditional MDBs should refocus their infrastructure strategies, with an emphasis on effective private-sector engagement and speed without cutting corners.* This should involve:

   a. Expanding and refining project preparation support.

   b. Developing innovative financial instruments to protect private-sector actors from risk.

   c. Enabling and supporting necessary political will at the highest levels.

   d. Building the capacity of foreign national and local governments to prepare and oversee bankable and replicable infrastructure projects.

   e. Evaluating existing project approval processes to determine and close gaps in efficiency.

Barriers to Bankable Infrastructure

Incentivizing Private Investment to Fill the Global Infrastructure Gap

Introduction

CONTEXT

On October 24, 2014, 21 Asian countries signed a memorandum of understanding creating the Asian Infrastructure Investment Bank (AIIB).[1] Now with 57 signatories, including prominent members of the Organization for Economic Cooperation and Development's Development Assistance Committee (OECD DAC), the AIIB will focus on large-scale infrastructure projects such as toll roads, power plants, seaports, and airports, "filling a gap left by other lending institutions."[2] The AIIB became operational on January 16, 2016. With an initial capitalization of $100 billion, it plans to invest between $2 billion and $5 billion in infrastructure in Asia in its first year.

World Economic Forum (WEF) data reveals that global infrastructure investment requires $3.7 trillion annually, but only $2.7 trillion is invested each year.[3] This annual gap of $1 trillion is often cited by the World Bank. A study by the Asian Development Bank (ADB) in 2009 estimates the infrastructure gap to be $8 trillion between 2010 and 2020 for Asia alone, with a need of about $750 billion per year in the region.[4] The large infrastructure gap means shortfalls in services and economic bottlenecks for billions of people globally, with especially profound gaps in Asia.

While different institutions define infrastructure in various ways, this report follows the WEF's definition and considers infrastructure as having economic and social components:

---

1. "The Memorandum of Understanding on Establishing the Asian Infrastructure Investment Bank (AIIB) Was Signed in Beijing–NEWS," Asian Infrastructure Investment Bank, http://www.aiibank.org/html/2015/NEWS _0408/1.html.

2. Ben Otto, "China-Led Bank to Focus on Big-Ticket Projects, Indonesia Says," *Wall Street Journal*, April 10, 2015, http://www.wsj.com/articles/china-led-aiib-to-focus-on-big-ticket-projects-indonesia-says-1428647276.

3. "The Global Infrastructure Gap," World Economic Forum, 2014, 14, http://reports.weforum.org/strategic -infrastructure-2014/introduction-the-operations-and-maintenance-om-imperative/the-global-infrastructure -gap/#view/fn-3.

4. "Infrastructure for a Seamless Asia," Asian Development Bank Institute, 2009, http://adb.org/sites /default/files/pub/2009/2009.08.31.book.infrastructure.seamless.asia.pdf.

- "Economic infrastructure: assets that enable society and the economy to function, such as transport (airports, ports, roads and railroads), energy (gas and electricity), water and waste, and telecommunications facilities

- Social infrastructure: assets to support the provision of public services, such as government buildings, police and military facilities, social housing, health facilities, and educational and community establishments."[5]

The emergence of the AIIB is an important issue for the traditional multilateral development banks (MDBs) such as the World Bank Group and U.S. government agencies that work on global infrastructure projects, including the U.S. Agency for International Development (USAID), the U.S. Trade and Development Agency (USTDA), the Overseas Private Investment Corporation (OPIC), and the U.S. Export-Import Bank (Ex-Im). With a new viable institution able to fund large infrastructure projects in developing countries, and perhaps fund and implement them more quickly, it is a time for reflection and action by these traditional entities.

There is a clear need for a greater pipeline of infrastructure projects, and funding must be leveraged from the private sector to achieve this. While there is willingness by private-sector actors to fill the global infrastructure gap with readily available finance, companies that seek to partner with development banks or U.S. agencies often face frustrations with long approval processes or perceive financial risk to be too high at various stages of a project.

Expanding and refining project preparation support, developing innovative financial tools to protect private-sector actors from risk, and building the capacity of foreign national and local governments to prepare and oversee bankable and replicable infrastructure projects will be important components of new strategies. Reform of the traditional ways of doing business is essential to build a pipeline of bankable infrastructure projects and ensure that citizens in Asia and globally have access to the quality infrastructure that enables healthy and productive lives.

OVERVIEW OF REPORT

This report provides background on the global infrastructure gap and explores the current state of play of the various public, private, and multilateral actors who work on infrastructure projects in the United States and globally. Two case studies of World Bank–funded infrastructure projects, in Mali and Cape Verde, illuminate the challenges related to financing and implementing infrastructure. Three important areas of needed reform are discussed: project preparation, product innovation, and foreign government capacity building. The report concludes with targeted recommendations for multilateral development banks and U.S. agencies that work on infrastructure, with a focus on creating an expanded pipeline of projects that are bankable for the private sector.

---

5. "The Global Infrastructure Gap," World Economic Forum, 7.

Background

THE GLOBAL INFRASTRUCTURE GAP

There has been a downward trend in the number of infrastructure projects and infrastructure project size in the last few years, despite an increase in the committed or announced spending of several bilateral and multilateral development institutions (see table 1).

Even with existing or announced increases, the funds from these institutions will not be enough to meet the estimated $1 trillion annual infrastructure gap. In 2014, combined multilateral and bilateral lending for infrastructure totaled around $130 billion, which is less than 15 percent of the gap.

Much of the downturn in infrastructure projects can be attributed to a decrease in private-sector spending in infrastructure following the 2008 global financial crisis, and the resulting lag in project initiation. Typically, it can take between two and five years to prepare an infrastructure project before implementation, or building, commences. The World Bank has seen renewed interest in private-sector investment in infrastructure in the past two to three years, but, as this report will discuss, reforms must translate this interest into physical projects that meet the needs of developing communities. Infrastructure experts agree that there are plentiful sources of capital for well-structured projects that effectively mitigate risks for investors, but these types of projects are difficult to come by.

THE IMPORTANCE OF INFRASTRUCTURE

In addition to yielding human development shortfalls, lack of quality infrastructure creates bottlenecks for economic growth in emerging economies. Gaps in infrastructure

Table 1. International Development Institution Spending on Infrastructure

Institution	2014 Spending on Infrastructure	Recent or Announced Changes in Spending on Infrastructure
World Bank[a]	$24.2 billion	Increased by 45 percent from 2013
ADB[b]	$15 billion; combined lending of $22–$23 billion	ADB announced plans to increase spending on private sector–related infrastructure activities from about 18 percent of its current total portfolio to 50 percent by 2020.
USAID	$632 million;[c] USAID also states that it spends "approximately $1 billion on infrastructure projects annually in conflict and crisis-affected countries."[d]	N/A
USTDA	$49 million (All of USTDA's program funds support infrastructure development.)[e]	N/A

(continued)

Table 1. (cont.)

Institution	2014 Spending on Infrastructure	Recent or Announced Changes in Spending on Infrastructure
Millennium Challenge Corporation (MCC)[f]	MCC only releases selected sector-specific data; in 2014, MCC spent ~$2.4 billion on road works and $574 million in water and sanitation works.[g]	In July 2015, MCC announced that it was committing an additional $70 million to project preparation—preparatory studies and due diligence—for public-private partnerships (PPPs) over the next five years. This is expected to catalyze $750 million in private investment for several kinds of PPPs, including those that aim to expand access to energy and water infrastructure.
Inter-American Development Bank (IDB)	$5.1 billion on infrastructure and environment sectors[h]	Spending accounts for 38 percent of total approvals, up from 34 percent in 2013.[i]
European Bank for Reconstruction and Development (EBRD)[j]	€1.3 billion (~$1.6 billion) on transport; €726 million (~$883 million) on municipal and environmental infrastructure[k]	Spending in 2014 increased from €1.1 billion on transport and €556 million on municipal and environmental infrastructure in 2013.[l]
OPIC[m]	2015 data—nearly $2 billion on infrastructure and energy sectors	OPIC experienced a record-setting portfolio of $20 billion in global projects in fiscal year 2015.
African Development Bank (AfDB)[n]	$3.5 billion	Spending increased from $2.8 billion in 2013.

a "World Bank Group's Infrastructure Spending Increases to US$24 Billion," World Bank, July 18, 2014, http://www.worldbank.org/en/news/press-release/2014/07/18/world-bank-group-infrastructure-spending-increases-to-24-billion.

b "2014 Annual Report," Asian Development Bank, April 2015, http://www.adb.org/sites/default/files/institutional-document/158032/adb-annual-report-2014.pdf.

c "Agency Financial Report Fiscal Year 2014," U.S. Agency for International Development, 2014, https://www.usaid.gov/sites/default/files/documents/1868/USAID_FY2014AFR.pdf.

d "Infrastructure," U.S. Agency for International Development, 2012, https://www.usaid.gov/what-we-do/economic-growth-and-trade/infrastructure.

e Correspondence with representatives of the U.S. Trade and Development Agency.

f "MCC pledges new PPP funding for project preparation," Devex, July 31, 2015, https://www.devex.com/news/mcc-pledges-new-ppp-funding-for-project-preparation-86626.

g "Agency Financial Report Fiscal Year 2014," Millennium Challenge Corporation, 2014, 19–20, https://assets.mcc.gov/reports/report-fy2014-afr.pdf.

h "2014 Annual Report," Inter-American Development Bank, March 18, 2015, https://publications.iadb.org/bitstream/handle/11319/6855/2014%20Annual%20Report.%20%20The%20Year%20in%20Review.pdf?sequence=13.

i "2013 Annual Report," Inter-American Development Bank, March 17, 2014, https://publications.iadb.org/bitstream/handle/11319/6422/IDB%20Annual%20Report%202013.%20%20The%20Year%20in%20Review.pdf?sequence=1.

j "Annual Report 2014," European Bank for Reconstruction and Development, May 14, 2015, http://www.ebrd.com/publications/annual-report.

k The conversions to U.S. dollars were achieved by using an exchange rate of $1.216 for €1. This exchange rate is used in "Annual Report 2014," European Bank for Reconstruction and Development, 15.

l "Annual Report 2013—Activities by Sector," European Bank for Reconstruction and Development, http://www.ebrd.com/downloads/research/annual/ar13ec.pdf.

m "OPIC announces record-setting year—Also achieves $4.4 billion in new commitments to catalyze private sector-led development," Overseas Private Investment Corporation, 2015, https://www.opic.gov/press-releases/2015/opic-announces-record-setting-year-44-billion-new-commitments-catalyze-private-sector-led-deve.

n "Annual Report 2014," African Development Bank Group, April 22, 2015, http://www.afdb.org/fileadmin/uploads/afdb/Documents/Generic-Documents/Annual_Report_2014_-Full.pdf.

stifle growth possibilities in both the short and medium term. The 2014 International Monetary Fund (IMF) *World Economic Outlook* reports that for low-income countries "the contemporaneous effect of a 1 percentage point of GDP [gross domestic product] increase in public investment is a 0.25 percent increase in output, which gradually increases to about 0.5 percent four years after the shock."[6] These effects vary with a variety of factors, including the efficiency of investment.

The 2014–2015 WEF "Global Competitiveness Report" includes infrastructure as one of its key pillars of competitiveness: "Extensive and efficient infrastructure is critical for ensuring the effective functioning of the economy, as it is an important factor in determining the location of economic activity and the kinds of activities or sectors that can develop within a country." In addition, quality infrastructure ensures connections to domestic and foreign markets and plays a key role in reducing income inequality and poverty.[7] No emerging economy appears on the WEF's list of top 10 countries in infrastructure competitiveness. Despite the demonstrated positive effects of public infrastructure spending, it has generally declined in both advanced and emerging economies since the 1970s and 1980s.

The importance of cities and countries having sufficient quality infrastructure will only continue to increase as urbanization accelerates. Currently more than 54 percent of the world's population resides in urban areas, and continuing population growth projects 2.5 billion people will be added to the urban population by 2050. In 15 years, the world will have 41 mega-cities with more than 10 million inhabitants each.[8] Capital cities such as Manila and Jakarta are already far behind on infrastructure that allows for adequate service delivery and the effective transportation of citizens and goods. These locations will need greater infrastructure investment from the public and private sectors in the coming years.

THE EMERGENCE OF THE ASIAN INFRASTRUCTURE AND INVESTMENT BANK (AIIB)

The emergence of the AIIB in 2014 led to a new international dialogue about the way international development is funded and what shortcomings exist in the current system. This discussion was largely driven by the fact that the AIIB is perceived as China-led because China is the AIIB's largest contributor and holds 26.06 percent of its voting share, thus giving it veto power on decisions that require a super majority.

Many traditional donor governments first viewed the AIIB with skepticism. One early concern was that the AIIB signaled China's desire to challenge the status quo of such Bretton Woods institutions as the World Bank Group with financing infrastructure projects that circumvent the high standards of these institutions. There is still a significant amount

---

6. "Is It Time for an Infrastructure Push? The Macroeconomic Effects of Public Investment," chapter 3 in *World Economic Outlook: Legacies, Clouds, Uncertainties*, International Monetary Fund, October 2014, http://www.imf.org/external/pubs/ft/weo/2014/02/pdf/c3.pdf.

7. Klaus Schwab, "The Global Competitiveness Report 2014–2015," World Economic Forum, 2014, 6, http://www3.weforum.org/docs/WEF_GlobalCompetitivenessReport_2014-15.pdf.

8. *World Urbanization Prospects: The 2014 Revision*, UN Department of Economic and Social Affairs, 2014, http://esa.un.org/unpd/wup/Highlights/WUP2014-Highlights.pdf.

of skepticism about whether the AIIB will do what it has set out to do while maintaining quality standards, but many stakeholders now see the AIIB as China's signal that it wants to be a bigger and more transparent part of the current institutional framework. Countries such as Germany, Australia, the United Kingdom, and Denmark are AIIB members.

The U.S. government initially expressed skepticism about the AIIB but recently changed its tone. After President Xi Jinping visited the United States in September 2015, the White House released a statement saying that the United States and China have committed to new financial institutions being "properly structured and operated in line with the principles of professionalism, transparency, efficiency, and effectiveness, and with the existing high environmental and governance standards."[9] However, it appears unlikely that the United States will join the AIIB.

Japan is also unlikely to join. In November 2015, it announced that it would reduce the time for loan approval from the Japan International Cooperation Agency (JICA) and the Japan Bank for International Cooperation (JBIC) from three years to between 18 months and two years. Japan also announced it would no longer require recipient government guarantees in all cases. Japan and the ADB have pledged $110 billion to develop and support Asian infrastructure in the next five years.[10]

When Germany announced it was joining the AIIB, its Ministry of Finance issued a press release stating: "In the German government's view, participating in the AIIB builds on Germany's successful involvement in international development banks and financial institutions for the purpose of supporting infrastructure projects."[11] The United Kingdom also mentioned positive impacts for the British economy: "The AIIB will help to finance vital infrastructure for the Asian and world economies. . . . Our involvement at its birth will help to unlock enormous opportunities for British companies and British jobs."[12]

The AIIB will have a unique opportunity to take the lessons learned of institutions such as the World Bank and the ADB after decades working on infrastructure and use these to inform more efficient ways of doing business. The hope here is that the AIIB will not discard the high standards that ensure environmental and social safeguards, but institute processes that reduce unnecessary lag time and effectively incentivize private-sector investment. Only a track record of complete projects spearheaded by the AIIB—which will take several years—will demonstrate whether this is the outcome. In any case, it is now

9. "FACT SHEET: U.S.-China Economic Relations," White House Office of the Press Secretary, September 25, 2015, https://www.whitehouse.gov/the-press-office/2015/09/25/fact-sheet-us-china-economic-relations.
10. David Tweed, "Abe Touts Streamlined Loans as China's AIIB Gets Set to Lend," Bloomberg News, November 21, 2015, http://www.bloomberg.com/news/articles/2015-11-21/abe-touts-streamlined-loans-as-china-s-aiib-gets-set-to-lend.
11. "German cabinet adopts legislation to join Asian Infrastructure Investment Bank," Germany Federal Ministry of Finance, September 2, 2015, http://www.bundesfinanzministerium.de/Content/EN/Pressemitteilungen/2015/2015-09-02-legislation-to-join-aiib.html.
12. "UK signs founding Articles of Agreement of the Asian Infrastructure Investment Bank," United Kingdom HM Treasury, June 29, 2015, https://www.gov.uk/government/news/uk-signs-founding-articles-of-agreement-of-the-asian-infrastructure-investment-bank.

time for the traditional development institutions working on infrastructure to examine and revise their internal processes.

CHALLENGES TO SUCCESSFUL AND EXPEDIENT INFRASTRUCTURE PROJECTS

One of the key challenges affecting infrastructure projects is speed. In many cases, this is fundamentally what a partner wants when collaborating with a U.S. agency or multilateral institution. Leaders of developing countries as well as multinational and local private-sector actors want to be involved in infrastructure projects that adhere to environmental and social safeguards, provide local capacity building, yield high-quality outcomes, and take shape in a reasonable amount of time.

However, completing high-quality projects in short time frames is not always an easy endeavor. Average project completion timelines are not readily available from U.S. agencies or multilateral institutions, but anecdotal evidence suggests that infrastructure projects often extend beyond their targeted completion dates. A 2014 review paper on the World Bank's public-sector management (PSM) portfolio notes that the average time for a non-PSM project to move from concept note to "effectiveness" or implementation is approximately two years and five months.[13] Some studies have been conducted on infrastructure initiatives in India, where 60 percent of projects are expected to suffer time and cost overruns, with an average delay of 20 to 25 percent beyond the scheduled timeline and budget.[14]

A specific example of an infrastructure project that faced considerable delays is the Bujagali Falls Dam in Uganda, which was scheduled to begin in January 2003. Instead, it was launched four years later due to resident protests and corruption investigations, and finally completed in 2012 with costs revised from $530 million to $900 million.[15] The gas pipeline and export facilities related to Camisea in Peru is another example. The IDB first delayed its vote on a $75 million dollar loan in 2003 due to environmental and social concerns raised by local and international nongovernmental organizations (NGOs).[16] More recently, the expansion of Peru's main pipeline was extended until 2016 due to threats posed by insurgents in the region.[17]

One reason for delays is the often time-consuming environmental and social impact evaluations that must be completed before a project is approved. Experts relate that the

13. Jürgen René Blum, "What Factors Predict How Public Sector Projects Perform? A Review of the World Bank's Public Sector Management Portfolio," World Bank Governance and Public Sector Management Practice, March 2014, https://openknowledge.worldbank.org/bitstream/handle/10986/17299/WPS6798.pdf?sequence=1.

14. Prashant Gupta, Rajat Gupta, and Thomas Netzer, "Building India—Accelerating Infrastructure Projects," McKinsey & Company, August, 2009, http://www.mckinsey.com/~/media/mckinsey%20offices/india /pdfs/building_india-accelerating_infrastructure_projects.ashx.

15. "Bujagali Falls Hydropower Dam, Jinja, Uganda," Power Technology, http://www.power-technology.com /projects/bujagali/.

16. Jim Lobe, "Bank Delays Vote on Controversial Peru Pipeline," July 30, 2003, http://www.ipsnews.net /2003/07/finance-bank-delays-vote-on-controversial-peru-pipeline/.

17. "Rebels delay finish of Peru natgas pipeline expansion until 2016," Reuters, October 14, 2014, http:// www.reuters.com/article/peru-pipeline-idUSL2N0S91TW20141014.

World Bank guidelines for addressing the involuntary displacements of individuals (adopted by other institutions such as the IDB) can be extremely onerous. One expert relayed that in his six years at the IDB, his division did not approve a single hydropower dam or new road for this reason.

Other challenges facing the efficient completion of infrastructure projects include difficulties with:

- Finding financial and other support for project preparation, including feasibility studies, detailed designs, and transaction structuring and bidding.

- The project's enabling environment, which sometimes includes too few local commercial banks able to provide financing in developing countries. This also can include political turnover that leads to gaps in political will. In some cases, changing administrations lead to gaps in government payments to cover operating expenses and debt service.

- Land acquisition processes.

One way of mitigating delays while ensuring that appropriate evaluations are completed is to incorporate them into project design, rather than first designing a project and then determining how it will affect the current environmental and social landscape in the target location. Several institutions, including the World Bank's Global Infrastructure Facility (GIF), already use this method.

PRIVATE-SECTOR INVOLVEMENT IN INFRASTRUCTURE

Infrastructure experts have noted that within the past two years across emerging markets, including Asia, governments have called for significantly greater scale in infrastructure projects, as well as more private capital to support them. Demands for energy capacity to be built in Indonesia, Brazil, Mexico, Bangladesh, and other locales in just the next five years outstrip the current energy capacity in those places.

These increased demands come at a time when U.S. companies have largely receded from global infrastructure financing in the past decade. There has also been a global decline in private-sector participation in infrastructure. According to the World Bank's "2014 Global PPI Update," private participation in infrastructure (PPI) in emerging markets reached $107.5 billion in 2014. This is 6 percent higher than the 2013 total, but significantly less than the 2012 total. Four of six world regions saw a decline in PPI in 2014 as compared to their five-year average from 2009 to 2013 (see table 2).[18]

Some of these declines can be attributed to the 2008 global financial crisis, but there are other considerations that determine the private sector's willingness to invest. While many private companies are looking to support infrastructure projects led by U.S. agencies and

---

18. "2014 Global PPI Update," World Bank, http://ppi.worldbank.org/~/media/GIAWB/PPI/Documents/Global -Notes/Global2014-PPI-Update.pdf.

Table 2. Investment by Region, 2014

	# of Projects	Total Investment (US$ billion)	% of Total Investment	% Change from 5-yr Average
LAC	110	69.1	64%	+53%
ECA	23	14.3	13%	−19%
EAP	46	11.5	11%	−13%
SAR	40	6.7	6%	−81%
MNA	13	3.3	3%	+60%
AFR	7	2.6	2%	−33%
Total	**239**	**107.5**	**100%**	**−9%**

Source: PPI Database, World Bank Group.

AFR, Africa; EAP, East Asia and Pacific; ECA, Europe and Central Asia; LAC, Latin America and the Caribbean; MNA, Middle East and North Africa; SAR, South Asia.

multilateral institutions with readily available capital, they have not always found a viable project pipeline. With most U.S. development funds going to Afghanistan, Pakistan, and Iraq, the basis on which to leverage private-sector capital for infrastructure in other countries of need is limited. The United States also faces criticism for having an outdated infrastructure finance model, one that is far behind countries in Asia. Infrastructure finance stakeholders additionally note that many of the staff in U.S. government or multilateral institutions charged with preparing bankable infrastructure projects for the private sector do not have the relevant private-sector or finance expertise to do so successfully. There is often a mismatch of expectations that leads to lost deals.

Another challenge facing private-sector actors who wish to invest in infrastructure is the mentality of some national and local governments that the public sector should take full responsibility for essential services—electricity, water, and others. Unfortunately, this mindset creates a culture where companies seeking to enter the public goods market are viewed with skepticism.

Another issue is the approach of multilateral development banks that have the mandate to "get money out the door." This approach is at odds with infrastructure projects, which typically are more expensive and time-consuming than other development projects. In addition, multilateral development banks sometimes monopolize the "low hanging fruits"—viable infrastructure projects appropriate for private sector investment—with their own project funding. This leaves higher-risk projects for the private sector, which in many cases is not willing to take on that level of risk.

Private-sector actors in infrastructure emphasize that there is plenty of capital, and many companies are actively looking for assistance to enter foreign markets. However, reforms are needed to attract these investments and make them viable and sustainable. Multilateral institutions and government agencies are arguably in the best position to match private capital with the knowledge, technology, and adequate risk allocation that enables it to achieve both sustainable and profitable returns and development impact.

Infrastructure Case Studies

METHODOLOGY

The following case studies feature two World Bank projects: Cape Verde's transport and infrastructure project and Mali's rural electrification hybrid system project. Data on these infrastructure projects was collected primarily through the World Bank's project database, with additional contextual information gathered through interviews with World Bank staff members.

CAPE VERDE: TRANSPORT AND INFRASTRUCTURE PROJECT

Key Facts

- The World Bank's transport and infrastructure project (TIP) in Cape Verde was approved in March 1993 and completed in June 2004.

- The project was funded by several international donors, including the Netherlands, Germany, the African Development Fund, the Arab Bank for Economic Development in Africa, and the Organization of Petroleum Exporting Countries (OPEC). The World Bank was the primary implementer.[19]

- Cape Verde's TIP had four goals: modernization of the marine ports, revitalization of the shipping industry, improvements to roadways, and capacity building in the Ministry of Transport and Communications (MoT).

- The TIP was completed after 11 years, extending 6 years and $10 million dollars beyond the original timeline and budget estimates.

- The scope and goals of the TIP changed several times during the implementation stage, which was partially responsible for the delay.

Background

Cape Verde spends nearly 15 percent of its gross domestic product (GDP) on infrastructure projects, approximately $147 million each year.[20] Relative to its neighbors on the coast of Africa and to more developed countries around the world, this figure is very high. Senegal spends just over 6 percent of its GDP on infrastructure, Ghana spends 7.5 percent, and the United States spends around 2.4 percent each year.[21] Over one third of Cape Verde's $147

---

19. "Implementation Completion Report (ICR) Review—Transport and Infrastructure Project," World Bank Group, 2005, http://lnweb90.worldbank.org/oed/oeddoclib.nsf/InterLandingPagesByUNID/8525682E0068603785 256F770048E694.

20. Cecilia M. Briceño-Garmendia and Daniel Alberto Benitez, "Cape Verde's Infrastructure: A Continental Perspective," World Bank Group, 2010, http://www.ppiaf.org/sites/ppiaf.org/files/publication/AICD-CapeVerde -Country-Report.pdf.

21. Clemencia Torres, Cecilia M. Briceño-Garmendia, and Carolina Dominguez, "Senegal's Infrastructure: A Continental Perspective," World Bank Group, 2011, http://elibrary.worldbank.org/doi/abs/10.1596/1813-9450 -5817; Vivien Foster and Nataliya Pushak, "Ghana's Infrastructure: A Continental Perspective," World Bank Group, 2011, http://water.worldbank.org/node/84000, Angie Schmitt, "The State of American Infrastructure

Downtown São Vicente, with a view of Porto Grande, Cape Verde's primary port for cruise ships and cargo

Source: ElsondeMadrid, "View of Downtown Mindelo, Baía do Porto Grande and Monte Cara," https://en.wikipedia.org /wiki/S%C3%A3o_Vicente,_Cape_Verde#/media/File:Cabo_2010_Monte_Cara.jpg.

million yearly expenditure is lost due to excessively high costs and operational inefficiencies in both the water and power sectors.[22] Because of geographical challenges that Cape Verde faces as a semi-arid island nation, power prices and water tariffs are significantly higher than anywhere else in Africa, despite a fairly well-developed infrastructure network. This makes further construction projects difficult and expensive.[23] Transportation-related infrastructure is especially important for the islands of Cape Verde, and while road density is relatively high and three quarters of roads are paved, more than half are in poor condition and need repairs.[24] Capacity building and the expansion of existing airports and sea ports is crucial for the continued economic prosperity of Cape Verde, as the island nation depends on significant trade with the African mainland, especially in potable water.[25]

The transport and infrastructure project (TIP) in Cape Verde initially involved four main components: modernization of the marine ports, a revitalization and modernization of the shipping industry, road improvements, and capacity building in the Ministry of Transport and Communications (MoT). The TIP's ultimate goal was to increase international competitiveness. The TIP initially also included a goal of developing offshore information industries, but this was dropped during the course of the project due to the global technological changes that made this industry obsolete. The project began with an approval

Spending in Four Charts," Streets Blog USA, May 21, 2015, http://usa.streetsblog.org/2015/05/21/the-state-of -american-infrastructure-spending-in-four-graphics/.
22. Briceño-Garmendia and Benitez, "Cape Verde's Infrastructure: A Continental Perspective."
23. Ibid., 1.
24. Ibid.
25. Ibid., 5.

date of March 1993, and was completed in June 2004. The primary funders of the TIP were the Netherlands, Germany, the African Development Fund, the Arab Bank for Economic Development in Africa, and the Organization of Petroleum Exporting Countries (OPEC).[26] The World Bank served as the primary implementer of the TIP.

The first objective, the modernization of Cape Verde's marine ports, was ambitious. The creation of two separate ports—one to handle passenger-related cruise services and the other for cargo shipments—was part of the TIP mission, but the performance of Cape Verde's existing ports was slower and less efficient than other West African ports, casting doubt on the usefulness of these new locations.[27] The management of all international ports in Cape Verde was handled by the National Port Authority.

Improvements to the existing roads in Cape Verde was a crucial component of the TIP. Since approximately half of existing roads in the country are in disrepair, building new roads would not solve the maintenance problem.[28] Restoration of extant roads was a primary mission of a separate government-sponsored infrastructure project that was established after the TIP was completed in 2004. During 2007, the road maintenance fund financed the building of more new roads, rather than completing repairs.[29] A more focused mission to the TIP, which specifically emphasized the importance of maintenance, might have created a stronger foundation for the road maintenance project's later work. Training and capacity building programs for the MoT that focus on project preparation and analyzing costs and benefits would have helped the road maintenance project evaluate which repairs are most urgent and how to best allocate funds to complete these projects.

Successes

At the project's inception, there was only one large Cape Verdean contractor established enough to contribute to the project. By the end of the project, however, three contractors from Cape Verde were involved. Encouraging local companies to hold a stake in the project implies that future infrastructure needs—for example, expansions or repairs on the TIP roads—will be handled by local contractors. The technical training programs provided by the World Bank equipped these Cape Verdean companies to handle the maintenance of TIP projects.

Challenges

While the goals of the TIP were straightforward, the program ran approximately $10 million over the World Bank's initial appraisal. Additionally, the TIP took 11 years from the proposal to completion, running 6 years behind schedule. This largely unexplained delay is

---

26. "Implementation Completion Report (ICR) Review—Transport and Infrastructure Project," World Bank Group.
27. Ibid., 7.
28. Briceño-Garmendia and Benitez, "Cape Verde's Infrastructure."
29. Ibid., 6.

one of the longest in World Bank history.[30] The World Bank granted four extensions to the program, but failed to enforce a reasonable timeline.

One of the factors that delayed the project was an "overly optimistic assessment of government capability" to address a project of this scale.[31] The inability to determine the requirements of the project ahead of time implies serious planning issues before the project launched. Because the World Bank creates country assistance strategy reports in order to guide objectives in any client country, concerns about the reliability or capabilities of the Cape Verdean government should have been included in that document and settled before the project broke ground.[32]

Despite the usually mild and dry climate in Cape Verde, adverse weather conditions required a segment of one of the project roads to be repaved. This cost the project significant time and money. A cushion for unforeseeable setbacks in the project's timeline and budget might have rectified the situation with less wasted time and money.[33] No further explanation was given for the "unforeseen climatic conditions" in any of the World Bank's records.[34]

Additions and changes to the scope of the project in the implementation stages rather than the project preparation stage made the TIP unwieldy and directionless. For example, in the first year of implementation, the World Bank added the construction of an airport on the island of São Vicente, ports in Boa Vista, Maio, and Porto de Furna, and the rehabilitation of the Porto Novo port. Later, the World Bank made the decision to forgo the development of an offshore information technology industry in Cape Verde because the development and spread of the Internet made that industry obsolete. These changes to the project mid-stream put the TIP over budget and caused some significant delays.[35]

Takeaways

The failures of the TIP are primarily a result of poor planning before the project itself began. The quality of the proposal was rated "satisfactory, but marginally so" by the World Bank.[36] The additions to the TIP during the implementation stage demonstrate that the original project's proposal was incomplete. It should have either included these additions from the beginning or created a separate project to ensure their completion. The World Bank's overestimation of the Cape Verdean government's abilities demonstrates the importance

---

30. "Implementation Completion Report (ICR) Review—Transport and Infrastructure Project," World Bank Group.

31. Ibid.

32. "Cape Verde—Country Partnership Strategy for the Period FY09–FY12," World Bank, 2009, http://documents.worldbank.org/curated/en/2009/03/10403884/cape-verde-country-partnership-strategy-period-fy09-fy12.

33. Ibid.

34. "Implementation Completion Report (ICR) Review—Transport and Infrastructure Project," World Bank Group.

35. Ibid., 4.

36. Ibid., 5.

of building government capacity within projects that require significant government input and responsibility, as was needed when changing the configurations and quantities of sea ports in the TIP.

MALI: RURAL ELECTRIFICATION HYBRID SYSTEM PROJECT

Key Facts

- The World Bank's rural electrification hybrid system project in Mali was proposed in 2013 and is scheduled to be completed in 2020.

- The project's main focus is to increase access to high-quality electricity services for the rural population of Mali through three goals: improving and expanding the use of existing electrical mini-grids, expanding the use of off-grid lighting markets, and building capacity to provide technical assistance.

- The rural electrification project holds great promise for Mali, especially because of its innovative and pragmatic approach, including providing solar lamps to households that are too remote for existing electrical grids to reach.

- Creating a productive dialogue with the Malian government is challenging in the wake of civil unrest and the resulting high government turnover rates.

Background

Currently, the estimated rate of access to electricity in Mali is 30 percent; it is as high as 55 percent in urban centers and as low as 15 percent in rural areas.[37] Urban electricity is provided by the state-owned national utility, Energie du Mali (EDM-SA), but the majority of the Malian population lives outside the EDM-SA coverage area.[38] About 80 percent of household energy in Mali is provided by burning wood or coal, which creates both an environmental and a health concern.[39] Women and children are disproportionately affected by the health impacts of biomass fuels due to indoor air pollution as well as the strain experienced by traveling far from home to collect wood due to deforestation. Wood-collecting time could otherwise be spent on schooling. Sometimes gender-based violence occurs when women and children travel long distances to collect wood.[40] Previously, government programs through EDM-SA succeeded in bringing electricity to more rural homes, but stopped short of tackling the immense energy shortage in the most rural areas due to the prohibitively high cost and low return on expanding existing grids.[41]

---

37. Fabrice Bertholet and Raluca Golumbeanu, "The Global Partnership on Output-Based Aid: Project Commitment Paper," October 1, 2013.
38. Ibid.
39. "Report No: PAD688," World Bank, November 15, 2013, http://www-wds.worldbank.org/external/default/WDSContentServer/WDSP/IB/2013/11/22/000356161_20131122125659/Rendered/PDF/PAD6880PAD0P130 10Box379866B00OUO090.pdf.
40. Ibid.
41. "Energie Du Mali SA," EDM-SA, accessed November 1, 2015, https://www.edm-sa.com.ml/.

Solar panels in rural Mali

Curt Carnemark, "ML032S03 World Bank," World Bank Photo Collection, August 14, 2008, https://flic.kr/p/5dokSt.

In December 2013, the World Bank proposed the rural electrification hybrid system project to expand access to electricity in rural parts of Mali. This project is slated for completion by September 2020. It is currently in the final stages of project preparation at the World Bank.[42] The projected total project cost is $45 million, with funding primarily from the International Development Association (IDA), the Global Partnership on Output-Based Aid, and the Strategic Climate Fund Grant.[43]

The rural electrification hybrid system project has three primary goals: improve and expand the use of existing electrical mini-grids, expand the use of off-grid lighting markets, and build capacity to provide technical assistance. Electrical mini-grids will allow for more access to renewable energy. This goal involves adding approximately 4.8 megawatts of capacity through hybrid electrical systems, including "photovoltaic panels, inverters, batteries and control electronics, and mini-grid extension and densification."[44] In order to screen potential contractors, the World Bank will be working with the Malian Agency for the Development of Household Energy and Rural Electrification (AMADER). The screening process guarantees that the contractors are reliable. Because the contractors are Malian businesses, it ensures that local companies will have a stake in the project's success and continuation.

The second objective is the expansion of off-grid lighting markets. In rural areas where expanding electrical grids is prohibitively expensive, the use of solar lanterns could replace traditional electric lighting. Solar lantern use encourages efficient and sustainable use of electricity where traditional grids cannot reach, while eliminating the harmful effects of biomass fuel.

---

42. "Mali Rural Electrification Hybrid System Project," World Bank, 2015, http://www.worldbank.org /projects/P131084?lang=en.
43. Ibid.
44. "Report No: PAD688," World Bank, November 15, 2013, http://www-wds.worldbank.org/external /default/WDSContentServer/WDSP/IB/2013/11/22/000356161_20131122125659/Rendered/PDF/PAD6880PAD0P130 10Box379866B00OUO090.pdf.

The final component of the project involves capacity building and technical assistance. The World Bank will support management of the new electrical systems, providing training, monitoring, and evaluation.

Successes

The major advantage of this project over other infrastructure projects in Mali is the bottom-up approach that involves local energy providers and operators. After a screening process by AMADER, the providers submitted independent proposals, which encouraged local private investment and involvement in the project from its inception. While the process might be slower than using foreign contractors, the benefits of local participation outweigh the time lost vetting proposals. Getting local players in the game is critical to a project's success and sustainability.

The high cost of expanding existing electrical networks, a challenge that other electrification projects encountered, is offset in this project by the money saved in providing solar lamps. Additionally, training programs to ensure that electricity use is properly monitored ensures that providers earn enough profit to continue using the new mini-grids. AMADER's involvement in this project enforces accurate and transparent monitoring of electricity usage and taxation, which keeps providers' and consumers' transactions honest and efficient.

Previous electrification efforts failed to address the rural dependency on petroleum, which is especially expensive and inefficient for land-locked countries like Mali. This project reduces that cost by installing hybrid mini-grids that use both solar power and diesel fuel.[45] Furthermore, the distribution of solar lamps in the most rural areas keeps diesel consumption and transportation costs down.

Challenges

The primary difficulty that this project has encountered so far stems from the 2012 civil unrest in Mali. It forced the World Bank to suspend funding for the project. Additionally, a large portion of AMADER and other government employees in Mali left office after the conflict, which meant that the relationships and agreements the World Bank had built with the local government needed reassessment.[46] Finally, the project preparation stage has taken more than two years, which suggests that either complications with the Malian government have impeded progress or that the World Bank has encountered some other challenge in planning for this project. Usually a project preparation stage does not last longer than two years for a World Bank project.[47] As of January 2016, the project is progressing as planned despite recent civil unrest that included the 2015 Bamako hotel attack.

---

45. Bertholet and Golumbeanu, "The Global Partnership on Output-Based Aid."
46. Ibid.
47. "Resource Guide: Project Cycle," The World Bank Group, 2015, http://go.worldbank.org/7TUC7LR960.

Takeaways

While in the early stages, this rural electrification project shows great promise. Encouraging local involvement through the use of local contractors ensures that the mini-grids are well maintained and continue to be effectively monitored by knowledgeable technicians. Hopefully, the extra time spent on project preparation will better equip the World Bank for challenges in the implementation stage, thus avoiding some of the problems that the Cape Verde TIP faced. Incorporating evaluations in the project preparation stage, as with the GIF, would encourage more rigorous planning during these early stages of the Mali rural electrification project.

Areas for Reform

PROJECT PREPARATION

Background

While the definition of project preparation varies across institutions, it is regarded as the critical first step of developing infrastructure projects. Project preparation typically involves at least some of the following components.[48]

- Developing approaches toward the **enabling environment** for an infrastructure project, including any regulations, laws, and institutions. This may also include local capacity and consensus building to ensure a project's effective implementation, replicability, and sustainability.

- **Defining a project**, including designing the basic project concept, identifying desired outcomes and potential partners, and conducting pre-feasibility studies that gauge the technical and financial challenges of implementing the project.

- Determining **project feasibility** through detailed social, financial, environmental, technical, and other relevant studies.

- **Structuring the project**, including assessing the appropriate mix of public and private partners and determining viable options for the financial, legal, and technical make-up of the project.

- **Achieving community buy-in** as soon as possible.

In some cases, project preparation may also encompass the following components, although these are typically left for the implementation stage.

- **Providing transaction support**, including overseeing the implementation of decided project financing, legal, and technical plans. This also involves managing procurement processes.

---

48. "ICA User Guide 2006—Infrastructure Project Preparation Facilities," Public-Private Infrastructure Advisory Facility, 2006, https://www.ppiaf.org/sites/ppiaf.org/files/publication/ICA%20Guide%202006%20-%20Infra%20Project%20Preparation%20-%20ENG.pdf.

- **Developing monitoring and evaluation plans** and implementing these where appropriate.

These activities may occur in various sequences, and as part of the activities of agencies, multilateral institutions, or specialized infrastructure project preparation facilities (IPPFs). Infrastructure stakeholders emphasize the importance of robust project preparation through public or donor funds to address the early-stage risks that can dissuade private-sector participation in infrastructure.

TRENDS AND GAPS

In the past 10 years at least 64 IPPFs (see appendix) have been operational with the aim of unlocking private-sector investment for infrastructure. The majority of these have developed since 2010 and focus on the following regions (see table 3):

Table 3. Regional Focus of IPPFs

Regional Focus	Number of IPPFs	Total Funds (US$)
Sub-Saharan Africa	18	~30 billion
Latin America and the Caribbean	7	~57 million
Middle East and North Africa	5	~453 million
South, East, and Southeast Asia	20	~58 billion
Global	14	~43 billion

Notable IPPFs include the following:

- The Asia Pacific Project Preparation Facility is a multi-donor trust fund established in 2014 with the support of Australia, Canada, and Japan. Its goal is to catalyze private-sector investment in infrastructure by providing financial assistance to member state governments in support of creating enabling environments, providing capacity building, and conducting legal, technical due diligence for project preparation and transaction structure. All Asian Development Bank (ADB) developing member countries are eligible for grants for projects in priority sectors, including climate resilience, sustainable development and regional economic integration, and proposals that enhance enabling reforms and government capacity development.[49]

- The EU-Africa Infrastructure Trust Fund (EU-AITF) aims to increase investment in infrastructure in sub-Saharan Africa by leveraging grants, long-term loan financing from development finance institutions, and coordination among European Union (EU) and non-EU donors for transport, energy, information and communications technology (ICT) and water sectors. Established in 2007 and supported by

---

49. "Asia Pacific Project Preparation Facility," Asian Development Bank, 2014, http://www.adb.org/documents /asia-pacific-project-preparation-facility.

thirteen entities, EU-AITF focuses on providing service in technical assistance, interest rate subsidies, investment grants, and financial instruments to deliver regional impact.[50]

- The World Bank's Global Infrastructure Facility (GIF) is a $100 million facility that became operational in August 2015 following the Addis Ababa Financing for Development Conference. Funders include the governments of Australia, China, Japan, Canada, and Singapore and the major multilateral development banks. The overall aim of the GIF is to increase private-sector involvement in infrastructure by providing technical assistance to private companies to help them enter new markets. The facility aims to do this while expediting processes without cutting corners. The first three years of the GIF are considered a "test run," with a projected eight to 10 "interventions" in energy, water and sanitation, transportation, and telecommunications.[51]

- GuarantCo was incorporated as a Mauritian company in 2005. Its sponsors include the United Kingdom's Department for International Development (DFID), the Ministry of Foreign Affairs of the Netherlands, the Netherlands Development Finance Company (Nederlandse Financierings-Maatschappij voor Ontwikkelingslanden N.V., or FMO), the Swiss Secretariat for Economic Affairs (SECO), the Swedish International Development Cooperation Agency (Sida), and the Private Infrastructure Development Group (PIDG). GuarantCo services as financier for local construction and infrastructure projects throughout sub-Saharan Africa.[52]

While there has been a boom in the number of these IPPFs and the funds available for project preparation in recent years, there is little known about the success and performance of these facilities. A June 2015 World Economic Forum (WEF) and Boston Consulting Group (BCG) report on IPPFs in Africa states that their performance has been poor overall, and the field is becoming more crowded and harder to navigate for those looking to enter the global infrastructure market.[53]

Infrastructure stakeholders note that with IPPFs, the devil is in the details. New players are welcome, but with new players come new challenges. There is uncertainty as to whether any of these IPPFs can adequately address the infrastructure gap. In many cases they are short-term facilities, but infrastructure is a long-term asset. In order to get the private sector on board as partners in infrastructure, facilities should establish and carry out procedures that exhibit accountability and add value. The WEF report recommends the following criteria for IPPFs:

---

50. "EU-Africa Infrastructure Trust Fund,"European Union Africa Infrastructure Trust Fund, Accessed November 1, 2015, http://www.eu-africa-infrastructure-tf.net/about/index.htm.
51. Author conversations with GIF staff, summer 2015.
52. "About GuarantCo," GuarantCo Ltd., 2015, http://www.guarantco.com/about-us.
53. "Africa Strategic Infrastructure Initiative: A Principled Approach to Infrastructure Project Preparation Facilities," World Economic Forum, June 2015, http://www3.weforum.org/docs/WEF_African_Strategic_Infrastructure_Initiative_2015_IPPF_report.pdf.

- "Clear objectives and a focused strategy;

- A self-sustainable financing model;

- Excellence in portfolio management;

- Cost-efficient and value-adding advisory services; and

- Stringent governance and accountability."[54]

A missing element of the WEF's recommendations is that IPPFs should also have a clear plan for what a project will accomplish and should consider how to galvanize local political will. Other suggestions from infrastructure stakeholders include that an IPPF provides grant money for project development and also emphasizes technical capacity building as part of its mandate. The Millennium Challenge Corporation (MCC), for example, includes funding in its compacts to embed highly competent transaction advisers in foreign governments in order to find and develop bankable projects.

These recommendations come down to the guiding principle that project preparation be demand driven. This means that it increases the capacity of local governments, improves the enabling environment for investment, and is private sector–led—it responds to where the private sector is interested to develop projects. Stakeholders emphasize the importance of involving the foreign and/or local private sector at the earliest stages of project preparation to achieve buy-in from the outset of the project design.

PRODUCT INNOVATION

Infrastructure stakeholders note that in addition to expanding and reforming project preparation, innovative financial products are needed. Multilateral development banks and government agencies should develop new instruments that address risks facing private-sector actors investing in infrastructure. Frustrated private-sector actors, who have an ample amount of money to invest in infrastructure, cannot find deals to invest in due to inadequate risk allocation. The current guarantees available are like drips in a well.

The innovation and evolution in both the public and private insurance industry has been largely stagnant for the last decade. The World Bank's Multilateral Investment Guarantee Agency (MIGA), for instance, has not initiated substantial changes to its political risk insurance (PRI) since the product was first offered. This product covers the investments of foreign direct investors from "transfer restriction, expropriation, war and civil disturbance, and breach of contract."[55]

---

54. Ibid., 7.
55. "WBG Guarantee Projects," World Bank, Accessed November 1, 2015, http://web.worldbank.org /WBSITE/EXTERNAL/EXTOED/EXTGUARANTE/0,,contentMDK:22082028~menuPK:5831687~pagePK:64829573~p iPK:64829550~theSitePK:4683335,00.html.

Other products offered by multilateral development banks and U.S. agencies include those outlined in table 4.

Private-sector actors would like to see the following kinds of guarantees added to the portfolios of more of these institutions:

- **Regulatory risk guarantees** addressing possible changes in regulation, including the addition of environmental safeguards, the revocation of licenses and permits, and price changes due to new government policies and tariffs.

- **Construction risk guarantees** that address the possible fluctuations in the timeline, bidding, and cost of construction projects, as well as other factors affecting a project's successful completion.

- **Market risk guarantees** addressing factors such as price distortion. Market risk especially affects water and sewage infrastructure projects, making them often unattractive for the private sector's involvement.

- **Guarantees for risk pushed to managers and operators**. Engineering, procurement, and construction (EPC) companies must be quasi-developed and include money for risk that does not include the consumer to be viable. These kinds of companies would like to see better credit offered to them for infrastructure deals by U.S. agencies and multilateral development banks. Companies note that Asian export credit agencies offer better credit than the U.S. Export-Import Bank, and they prefer to partner with Asian companies in Asia for this reason.

- **Credit enhancement**, which reduces the risk of a transaction by providing "support to a project's cash flows . . . augmenting its ultimate ability to retire debt by enhancing its current ability to meet debt service requirements. This mitigation of default risk, where the project has ample ability to ultimately retire its debt, can lift the credit quality of a project, making it more acceptable with respect to the investment criteria of institutional funds"[56]

FOREIGN GOVERNMENT CAPACITY BUILDING

Infrastructure stakeholders note that there is a strong correlation between a location's enabling environment and the prevalence and quality of infrastructure in that place. Weak government capacity and an inefficient legal system create implications for project initiation, scale-up, and sustainability. Losses due to corruption in developing countries can amount to between 10 to 30 percent of an infrastructure project's value,[57] and this can dissuade investors. Stakeholders note the need for a policy environment that ensures a project survives the test of time. It is important not only to put in place a policy that enables

---

56. William Streeter, "Credit Enhancement: The Missing Link in Infrastructure Finance," Stanford Global Projects Center, July 29, 2014, https://gpc.stanford.edu/sites/default/files/wp085_0.pdf.

57. Jenna Carter, "Infrastructure is costly but necessary to development: Transparency is a must," ONE, September 30, 2011, http://www.one.org/us/2011/09/30/infrastructure-is-costly-but-necessary-to-development-transparency-is-a-must/.

Table 4. International Development Institution Guarantee Products

Institution	Guarantee Product	Description
World Bank (of World Bank Group)	Partial Credit Guarantee (PCG)	Provided for commercial lenders or government bond issues to provide comprehensive coverage against all risks; this includes policy-based guarantees (PBG) that support general policy reforms rather than specific projects.[a]
	Partial Risk Guarantee (PRG)	Provided for commercial lenders against a government-owned entity failing to perform obligations in a private-sector project: either due to changes in law, failure to meet payment obligations, expropriation and nationalization,[a] etc.
International Finance Corporation (of World Bank Group)	Direct Debt Substitutes	Provided to either a single or portfolio of credits, promising a predetermined amount irrespective of the cause of default.[a]
	Commercial Operation	Provided to a non-lending situation, such as a transaction that involves the provision of goods and services, through guarantes of bid or performance bonds (otherwise known as standby letters of credit).[a]
	Global Trade Finance Program (GTFP)	Provides partial or full guarantees to banks to enhance import and export trade transactions, and can extend to both political and commercial risks.[a]
	Global Offshore Liquidity (GOLF)	Provides single risk coverage for transfer and convertibility risk.[a]
European Bank for Reconstruction and Development	Risk Sharing on Portfolio Basis	Provided to partner banks on certain portfolios for coverage against default regardless of the cause.[b]
	Risk Sharing of Specific Exposures	Provided to partner banks for coverage against default arising from specified events.[b]
	Trade Facilitation Program	Provided to banks for coverage of political and commercial payment risk of international trade transactions.[c]
Asian Development Bank	Political Risk Guarantee (PRG)	Provided for commercial lenders for coverage against specifically defined political or sovereign risks including: transfer restriction, expropriation, political violence, contract disputes, and non-honoring of a sovereign obligation.[d]
	Partial Credit Guarantee (PCG)	Provided for lenders of most forms of debt, principally in the financial services and capital markets (e.g., banking, leasing, insurance, and funds), and in infrastructure development projects.[d]
	Credit Guarantee and Investment Facility (CGIF)	Provides guarantees for local currency denominated bonds issued by investment-grade companies in Association of Southeast Asian Nations (ASEAN+3) countries, to support financial stability and long-term investment.[e]

Institution	Guarantee Product	Description
African Development Bank	Partial Risk Guarantee (PRG)	Provided for private lenders against the failure of a government or related entity to honor commitments; such political risks include: political force majeure, currency inconvertibility, changes in law, breach of contract.[f]
	Partial Credit Guarantee (PCG)	Provided for coverage against development projects in low-income countries that are classified with low risk of debt distress.[f]
Inter-American Development Bank	Credit Guarantee	Provided for private and sub-national entities and can include coverage for all risks for selected terms of a loan made by a commercial lender.[g]
	Political Risk Guarantee	Provided for private and sub-national entities for coverage against political risks, including: breach of contract, currency convertibility and transferability.[g]
Overseas Private Investment Corporation	Investment Guarantees to Third Party Lenders	Provided for a third-party (non-OPIC) lender against risk of default from the borrower.[h]
	Political Risk Insurance	Provided for U.S. investors, lenders, contracts, exporters, and NGOs for investments for coverage against political risks, including: politically motivated violence, expropriation and improper host government interference, restrictions on currency convertibility and transferability.[i]
United States Agency for International Development	Development Credit Authority	Provides assurance through four types of guarantee products: loan guarantees, loan portfolio guarantees, leasing portfolio guarantees (e.g., issued to qualifying leasing companies to enable farmers to access equipment), and bond guarantees on corporate or sub-sovereign bond issuance.[j]

[a] "WBG Guarantee Projects," World Bank, Accessed November 1, 2015, http://web.worldbank.org/WBSITE/EXTERNAL/EXTOED/EXTGUARANTE/0,,contentMDK:22082028~menuPK:5831687~pagePK:64829573~piPK:64829550~theSitePK:4683335,00.html.

[b] "Guide to EBRD Financing," European Bank for Reconstruction and Development, 2013, http://www.ebrd.com/downloads/research/factsheets/guidetofinancing.pdf.

[c] "Trade Facilitation Programme," European Bank for Reconstruction and Development, Accessed November 1, 2015, http://www.ebrd.com/work-with-us/trade-facilitation-programme.html.

[d] "Guarantees," Asian Development Bank, Accessed November 1, 2015, http://www.adb.org/site/private-sector-financing/commercial-cofinancing/guarantees.

[e] "Credit Guarantee and Investment Facility (CGIF)," Asian Development Bank, Accessed November 1, 2015, http://www.adb.org/site/funds/funds/credit-guarantee-and-investment-facility.

[f] "Guarantees," African Development Bank Group, Accessed November 1, 2015, http://www.afdb.org/en/projects-and-operations/financial-products/african-development-fund/guarantees/.

[g] "Guarantees," Inter-American Development Bank, Accessed November 1, 2015, http://www.iadb.org/en/about-us/idb-financing/guarantees-,6040.html.

[h] "Products," Overseas Private Investment Corporation, Accessed November 1, 2015, https://www.opic.gov/what-we-offer/financial-products/products.

[i] "Political Risk Insurance," Overseas Private Investment Corporation, Accessed November 1, 2015, https://www.opic.gov/what-we-offer/political-risk-insurance.

[j] "Impact Brief 2013," Development Credit Authority, 2013, https://www.usaid.gov/sites/default/files/documents/2151/2013ImpactBrief.pdf.

implementation of a specific project, but also one that allows for its replication, especially through standardization and simplification of documentation. This is critical to moving the development needle beyond a project-by-project focus.

The enabling environment plays a large role in the private sector's decision of whether or not to invest in an infrastructure project. The World Bank conducts annual investor surveys in weaker emerging markets and asks what investors care about the most.[58] The top response has always been legal redress protection for investors. In many cases, politics comes as the top deal breaker for companies. Private-sector actors see local political will and clear leadership around an agenda or a project as one of the top determinants of success of an infrastructure project. Accordingly, they often consider the time remaining until the next election when deciding whether or not to invest. Three to four years is considered a sufficient time frame. If there is political turnover and the next administration or relevant leader no longer supports the project, it may be dead in the water. A key part of the preparation for an infrastructure project should involve determining how to engage local decision makers and influence them to make key decisions expediently.

Training a cadre of government officials as able counterparts early on is also cited as an important ingredient in enabling environments that provide for robust quality infrastructure. A key issue has been the institutional capacity of ministries. Stakeholders note that government officials do not have the capacity to effectively work with the private sector. Competent ministers want objective advice on which IPPF makes the most sense for what they are trying to get done and on which projects are good long-term investments.

An example of an IPPF that builds local capacity in deal structuring is the African Legal Support Facility (ALSF). Created by the African Development Bank in 2010, this facility supports African governments through commercial transactions with international investors.[59] By providing legal advice and technical assistance to local lawyers, the ALSF helps African governments in crafting and negotiating strong contracts and concessions. The thinking behind the creation of the facility was that increased local capacity and improved legal representation would secure stronger contracts and more effective international negotiations. The ALSF currently assists in 26 different projects, 70 percent of which are related to the training and support of government officials.

The importance of building a strong legal and regulatory framework for investment is especially high in Africa. Power Africa, a U.S. Presidential Initiative initiated in June 2013 that seeks to bring 10,000 megawatts of power and 20 million new connections to citizens in Ethiopia, Ghana, Kenya, Liberia, Nigeria, and Tanzania,[60] found that there were not near

---

58. Laura Gómez-Mera, Thomas Kenyon, Yotam Margalit, José Guilherme Reis, and Gonzalo Varela, "New Voices in Investment: A Survey of Investors in Emerging Countries," World Bank, 2015, http://www.worldbank.org/content/dam/Worldbank/document/Trade/New_Voices_in_Investment.pdf.

59. "African Legal Support Facility," African Development Bank Group, 2016, http://www.afdb.org/en/topics-and-sectors/initiatives-partnerships/african-legal-support-facility/.

60. U.S. Agency for International Development Report to Congress on Power Africa, USAID, July 20, 2015, https://www.usaid.gov/sites/default/files/documents/1860/PowerAfricaReport-FY2015.pdf.

enough transactions in the target countries there to meet the project's goals. These six initial countries were chosen on the grounds that they have demonstrated strong political will to pursue reforms,[61] but gaps remain. Power Africa staff members are in intelligence-gathering mode now to determine the cause of the shortage. Developing a project pipeline is now a core component of Power Africa. Transaction advisers are embedded in government ministries to promote a stronger enabling environment for deals to occur.

Stakeholders assert that U.S. agencies and the traditional multilateral development banks are in a strong position to offer more of the training and technical assistance that local governments desire. While budgetary restraints must be considered, this is the part of the equation that requires the least amount of spending, and it is where these actors can respond most effectively.

Training and technical assistance is also where these actors can present a more salient alternative to projects conducted with less rigorous standards. Stakeholders note that Chinese infrastructure projects in Africa typically involve Chinese workers completing the projects themselves, thus they are not building local capacity. However, African governments are looking to boost their own capacity; they want the training and technology to build and run their own projects over time. This is something that the Asian Infrastructure and Investment Bank (AIIB) will need to take into account when it begins its operations. Without a strong enabling environment, even the AIIB will not be able to deliver on infrastructure.

Recommendations

1. *The United States should pursue a strategic development and infrastructure finance agenda alongside its trade agenda in the Asia region, and take a stronger approach in emphasizing U.S. comparative advantages.* This should involve:

   a. Launching a major new initiative in collaboration with Japan and other allies to strengthen the Asian Development Bank (ADB). ADB's president Takehiko Nakao has demonstrated excellent leadership thus far, and his recommendation for strengthening the ADB should be supported, especially in light of the fact that the U.S. government will not join the AIIB. The U.S. government should call for a capital increase for the 2016–2018 period and expanded ADB lending capability. ADB's capability to prepare bankable infrastructure deals can also be improved with current resources.

   b. Expanding and refining global project preparation support, especially by strengthening the U.S. Trade and Development Agency (USTDA). USTDA has 30 years of experience in project preparation and documented success in completing high-quality infrastructure projects. The U.S. government should consider doubling the budget allocated to USTDA.

---

61. Jennifer G. Cooke, "Power Africa's Balancing Act," Center for Strategic and International Studies, June 30, 2015, http://csis.org/publication/power-africas-balancing-act.

c. Reducing the time for loan approval. Following the lead of the Japan Bank for International Cooperation (JBIC) and the Japan International Cooperation Agency (JICA), U.S. agencies should reduce the time for loan approval to a maximum of two years and no longer require guarantees from developing country recipient governments in all cases.

d. Providing technical training and knowledge transfers in each of its infrastructure projects. This is the area in which the U.S. government holds comparative advantage over newer institutions, and it is also the area in which it can have the most impact while spending the least funds. Capacity building of local or national foreign government officials should be a key stated objective in every infrastructure project the U.S. government funds.

2. *The traditional multilateral development banks (MDBs) should refocus their infrastructure strategies, with an emphasis on effective private-sector engagement and speed without cutting corners.* This should involve:

a. Expanding and refining project preparation support. Project preparation should involve the private sector at the earliest possible stage to co-design projects and be demand driven. Project preparation is also the point at which necessary evaluations should take place, thus avoiding unnecessary delays at later stages.

b. Developing innovative financial instruments to protect private-sector actors from risk. As with reforms to project preparation, these innovations should be demand driven and respond to what the private sector needs in order to have adequate risk allocation in its investments.

c. Building the capacity of foreign national and local governments to prepare and oversee bankable and replicable infrastructure projects. This should be initially contained in the project preparation stage of the project, with technical assistance and knowledge transfers occurring throughout project implementation. In particular, leaders in government ministries responsible for sourcing and preparing infrastructure deals and project procurement officers should receive training. This training should include instruction on all aspects of project preparation and deal-making, as well as assistance forming connections with the local private sector to understand needs and ways of doing business. It is also important that transaction advisers be embedded in foreign government counterpart offices.

d. Enabling and supporting necessary political will at the highest levels. This should also be initially contained in the project preparation stage of the project and cultivated throughout a project's life span. Galvanizing political will ensures a strong local champion paves the way for project success and sustainability.

e. Evaluating existing project approval processes to determine and close gaps in efficiency. MDBs should take a close look at what bottlenecks are causing delays in project approval for infrastructure, be transparent about average project completion time frames, and implement reforms toward achieving the goal that approvals take no more than two years across all projects. The government of Japan's new infrastructure strategy is a good model for consideration, and MDBs should also ensure that time-consuming evaluations, such as those that weigh the impacts of a proposed project on indigenous peoples or the environment, are always conducted in the project design or pre-planning stage.

Conclusion

As the Mali and Cape Verde case studies demonstrate, infrastructure is a topic that holds real implications for the livelihoods and living conditions of billions of people in developing countries around the world. People suffer when a road is not built that could take their goods to market; when energy access is not extended to their homes in rural areas that would allow their children to complete homework at nighttime; or when a planned infrastructure project goes 10 years beyond schedule and delays a better source of local fuel. U.S. government and MDBs responsible for pursuing infrastructure projects should, and can, do better.

With a global infrastructure gap of $1 trillion annually, capital must be drawn from the private sector. However, in the current environment, companies express frustration that there is not a robust pipeline of infrastructure deals with adequate risk allocation in which to invest ready funds. Tapping into this capital requires a mind-set revision and a behavior change by public and MDB officials. They should learn to understand what makes a deal bankable in the eyes of the private sector. Refining project preparation to involve the private sector at the outset and providing innovative financial products that address various project risks are essential to creating a bankable pipeline of deals.

Finally, as the ultimate goal should not just be single project completion, but rather achieving sustainable development impact, it is not good enough that a project happens once. Infrastructure projects must incorporate local capacity building and local ownership, so that deals are replicable. Training a cadre of local government officials throughout the timeline of a project will go far in encouraging subsequent locally driven projects with effective engagement of the local private sector. This will be a key piece in both closing the global infrastructure gap and moving the development needle from projects being United States or MDB led, to projects being locally led.

Appendix. Infrastructure Project Preparation Facilities (IPPFs)

Sixty-four IPPFs are listed by regional focus. Please note that this may not be an all-inclusive listing of IPPFs.

Global Facilities (14)

- U.S. Trade and Development Agency (USTDA)

- Clean Technology Fund (CTF)

- Energy Sector Management Assistance Program (ESMAP)

- Global Infrastructure Facility (GIF)

- Global Infrastructure Hub

- Global Partnership on Output-Based Aid (GPOBA)

- Global Road Safety Facility (GRSF)

- IFC Asset Management Company (AMC) Catalyst Fund

- IFC Asset Management Company (AMC) Global Infrastructure Fund

- InfraVentures

- Infrastructure Development Collaboration Partnership Fund (DevCo)

- New Development Bank

- Public-Private Infrastructure Advisory Facility (PPIAF)

- Scaling Up Renewable Energy (SREP)

Latin America and the Caribbean (7)

- Brazil Private Sector Participation (PSP) Development Program
- Brazilian Project Structuring Company (Estruturadora Brasileira de Projetos, EBP)
- Fund for Integration Infrastructure (Fondo de Infraestructuras de Integración, FIRII)
- Infrastructure Fund (InfraFund)
- Project Structure Fund (Fundo de Estruturaqdo de Projetos, FEP)
- Regional Public-Private Partnerships (PPP) Support Facility
- Special Broadband Program

Sub-Saharan Africa (18)

- Africa Infrastructure Program (AIP)
- Africa50 Infrastructure Fund
- African Water Facility (AWF)
- DBSA EIB Project Development and Support Facility
- Emerging Africa Infrastructure Fund
- EU-Africa Infrastructure Trust Fund (EU-AITF)
- Green Africa Power
- GuarantCo
- InfraCo Africa
- Infrastructure Consortium for Africa (ICA)
- Infrastructure Crisis Facility–Debt Pool
- Infrastructure Project Preparation Facility (IPPF)
- Program for Infrastructure Development in Africa (PIDA)
- Project Preparation and Implementation Unit (PPIU)
- Project Preparation Development Fund (PPDF)
- Project Preparation and Development Facility (PPDF)
- Sustainable Energy Fund for Africa (SEFA)
- Technical Assistance Facility

East, South, and Southeast Asia (20)

- Adapt Asia-Pacific
- ASEAN Infrastructure Centre of Excellence
- Asia Infrastructure Centre of Excellence (AICOE)
- Asia Infrastructure Investment Bank (AIIB)
- Asia Pacific Project Preparation Facility (AP3F)
- Cities Development Initiative for Asia (CDIA)
- Clean Energy Financing Partnership Facility (CEFPF)
- GuarantCo
- India Infrastructure Project Financing Facility (IIPFF)
- Accelerating Infrastructure Investment Facility in India (AIIFI)
- InfraCo Asia
- JICA Preparatory Survey (JPS)
- JICA Preparatory Survey for PPP Infrastructure (JPSPI)
- JICA Technical Cooperation for Development Planning (JTCDP)
- Philippines Project Development and Monitoring Facility (PDMF)
- Project Preparation and Start-up Support Facility (PPSSF)
- Public-Private Partnership Support Project
- Sustainable Transport Initiative (STI)
- Technical Assistance Facility
- Urban Development Financing Partnership Facility (UDFPF)
- Water Financing Partnership Facility (WFPF)

Middle East, North Africa, Europe, and Eurasia (5)

- Arab Financing Facility for Infrastructure (AFFI)
- European Bank for Reconstruction & Development (EBRD) Infrastructure Project Preparation Facility

- Sustainable Energy Initiative (SEI)

- The Facility for Euro-Mediterranean Investment and Partnership Trust Fund (FEMIP Trust Fund; sometimes referred to as FTF)

- The Far East and Baikal Region Development Fund (FEDF)

About the Project Director and Authors

Daniel F. Runde is director of the Project on U.S. Leadership in Development and the Project on Prosperity and Development and holds the William A. Schreyer Chair in Global Analysis at CSIS. His work centers on leveraging American soft power instruments and the central roles of the private sector and good governance in creating a more free and prosperous world. Previously, he led the Foundations Unit for the Department of Partnerships & Advisory Service Operations at the International Finance Corporation. His work facilitated and supported over $20 million in new funding through partnerships with the Bill and Melinda Gates Foundation, Rockefeller Foundation, Kauffman Foundation, and Visa International, among other global private and corporate foundations.

Earlier, Mr. Runde was director of the Office of Global Development Alliances at the U.S. Agency for International Development (USAID). He led the initiative by providing training, networks, staff, funds, and advice to establish and strengthen alliances, while personally consulting to 15 USAID missions in Latin America, the Middle East, and Africa. His efforts leveraged $4.8 billion through 100 direct alliances and 300 others through training and technical assistance. Mr. Runde began his career in financial services at Alex. Brown & Sons, Inc., in Baltimore and worked for both CitiBank and BankBoston in Buenos Aires, Argentina. He received an M.P.P. from the Kennedy School of Government at Harvard University and holds a B.A., cum laude, from Dartmouth College.

Helen Moser is a research fellow with the Project on U.S. Leadership in Development and the Project on Prosperity and Development at CSIS. Her research interests include good governance approaches, private-sector engagement in international development, and women's political participation. Prior to joining CSIS, she conducted research with the Brookings Institution on shared value approaches in the public-private partnerships of the U.S. Agency for International Development. She has also worked with the Georgetown Institute for Women, Peace, and Security; Save the Children, in Sri Lanka; Vital Voices Global Partnership; and the Asian University for Women, in Bangladesh. Her experience additionally includes positions in the nonprofit and public sectors in the Federated States of Micronesia, Germany, Scotland, and Taiwan. She is a Phi Beta Kappa graduate of the University of Southern California and holds a master's in global human development from Georgetown University's School of Foreign Service.

Erin Nealer is a research assistant with the Project on U.S. Leadership in Development at CSIS. Previously, she was a research associate at Babson Global and the Asian Development Bank. She holds a B.A. from Wellesley College.